IR

# DENVER
# NUGGETS

by Brian Howell

Published by ABDO Publishing Company, 8000 West 78th Street, Edina, Minnesota 55439. Copyright © 2012 by Abdo Consulting Group, Inc. International copyrights reserved in all countries. No part of this book may be reproduced in any form without written permission from the publisher. SportsZone™ is a trademark and logo of ABDO Publishing Company.

Printed in the United States of America,
North Mankato, Minnesota
062011
092011

Editor: Matt Tustison/Dave McMahon
Copy Editor: Nick Cafarelli
Series design and cover production: Christa Schneider
Interior production: Carol Castro

**Photo Credits:** Jack Dempsey/AP Images, cover; Tim DeFrisco/Getty Images, 1, 28; Gary Stewart/AP Images, 4; David Zalubowski/AP Images, 7, 8, 38, 41, 43 (bottom); George Gojkovich/Getty Images, 10; AP Images, 12, 42 (top); SC/AP Images, 15, 42 (middle); Mark Duncan/AP Images, 16; Larry C. Morris/Getty Images, 19; Lennox McLendon/AP Images, 21; Stephen Dunn/Getty Images, 22, 43 (top); Ed Andrieski/AP Images, 24, 47; Don Emmert/AP Images, 27, 42 (bottom); Mark Lennihan/AP Images, 31; Darron Cummings/AP Images, 33; Kevork Djansezian/AP Images, 34, 43 (middle); Steve Yeater/AP Images, 37; Nathan Denette/AP Images, 44

**Library of Congress Cataloging-in-Publication Data**
Howell, Brian, 1974-
 Denver Nuggets / by Brian Howell.
   p. cm. -- (Inside the NBA)
 Includes index.
 ISBN 978-1-61783-155-3
 1.  Denver Nuggets (Basketball team)--History--Juvenile literature.  I. Title.
 GV885.52.D46H69 2012
 796.323'640978883--dc23
                        2011020392

# TABLE OF CONTENTS

Chapter 1 ............. The Upset, 4

Chapter 2 ............. Rockets Launch, 10

Chapter 3 ............. Joining the NBA, 16

Chapter 4 ............. Moe's Team, 22

Chapter 5 ............. The Lean Years, 28

Chapter 6 ............. "Melo" Arrives, 34

Timeline, 42

Quick Stats, 44

Quotes and Anecdotes, 45

Glossary, 46

For More Information, 47

Index, 48

About the Author, 48

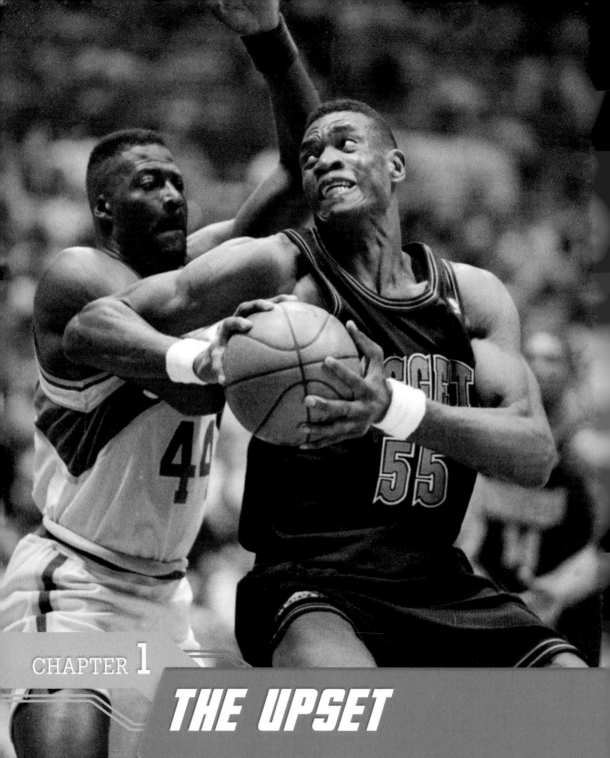

CHAPTER 1

# THE UPSET

**D**ikembe Mutombo snagged the ball out of the air, held it tight, and flashed a bright smile. When the final buzzer sounded, Mutombo fell to the ground and, smiling brighter than ever, hoisted the ball in the air.

On that day, May 7, 1994, Mutombo and the Denver Nuggets shocked the Seattle SuperSonics. Denver's 98–94 overtime victory in Game 5 of the first round of the Western Conference playoffs gave the Nuggets the series win. The National Basketball Association (NBA) went to eight-team conference playoffs beginning in the 1983–84 season. Denver's victory marked the first time that a team seeded eighth had eliminated a number one seed.

Although the Nuggets have never won a league championship, they have enjoyed many great moments through the

The Nuggets' Dikembe Mutombo (55) spins around Seattle's Michael Cage during the 1994 Western Conference playoffs.

years. The series win over the SuperSonics in 1994 might be the most exciting.

Still, success did not come easily for the 1993–94 Nuggets. When the regular season ended, Denver barely had a winning record at 42–40. The Nuggets finished eighth out of 13 teams in the Western Conference. As the 1994 playoffs began, Denver looked like any other number eight seed had in previous years. After all, their opponent was the top-seeded SuperSonics. Seattle had the best record in the NBA, 63–19. The Nuggets were not given much of a chance to win.

In the best-of-five series, the first team to get to three victories would win the series. Game 1 in Seattle went as expected, with the Sonics cruising to a 106–82 victory. Seattle also won Game 2, 97–87. All the SuperSonics had to do was win one of the final three games to move on to the second round. It is possible that Seattle looked ahead too soon.

"The first game was a throwaway. It might have worked to our advantage because Seattle might have thought it was going to be a short series," Denver coach Dan Issel said.

The Nuggets fought back to win Game 3. Reggie Williams

LaPhonso Ellis played a key role in helping the Nuggets knock out the top-seeded Seattle SuperSonics in the 1994 NBA playoffs.

and Mutombo had outstanding games in the Nuggets' 110–93 home victory. In Game 4, big men LaPhonso Ellis and Mutombo dominated to help Denver prevail 94–85 in overtime. That tied the series and sent it to a winner-take-all Game 5 in Seattle.

Denver was the youngest club in the NBA that season, but

### Waiting for a Winner

*When the Nuggets defeated the Sonics in the 1994 playoffs, it was their first postseason series win since 1988—when they also beat the SuperSonics. The Nuggets had lost three playoff series in the years between.*

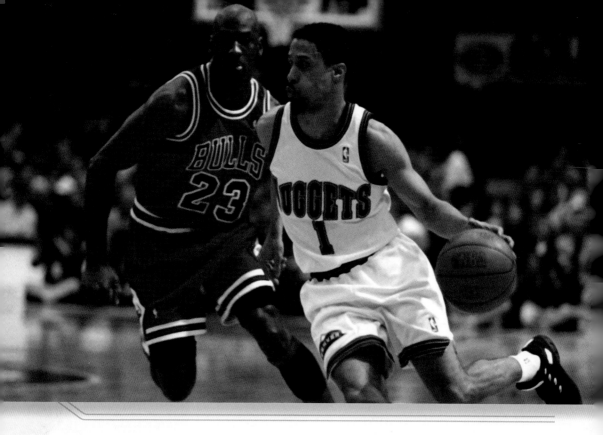

Nuggets guard Mahmoud Abdul-Rauf, *right*, works the ball past the Chicago Bulls' Michael Jordan in February 1996.

the Nuggets went into Game 5 confident. "I don't think our kids knew they were supposed to be nervous," Issel said.

Facing the prospect of an upset loss, it was the Super-Sonics who got nervous. Even Seattle coach George Karl could feel it. Karl, who later coached the Nuggets, said, "I can't deny the butterflies felt like rocks."

Seattle actually needed a miracle just to force overtime in Game 5. Kendall Gill made a last-second layup to tie the score for the Sonics. But in overtime, the Nuggets prevailed. In that game, most of the Nuggets' best players—Mutombo, Ellis, Robert Pack, Reggie Williams, Brian Williams, Bryant Stith, and Mahmoud Abdul-Rauf—

provided pivotal points, rebounds, or assists. Mutombo's rebound on the last play was his 15th of the game. When the 7-foot-2 center grabbed that ball, he secured the Nuggets' remarkable series win. The sheer joy on his face expressed that the victory was truly remarkable.

The Nuggets had missed the postseason three years in a row before qualifying in 1994. "We've come a long way, and to be honest, we just wanted to get some playoff experience this year," Issel said. "Getting this much is a bonus."

During the next round of the playoffs, the Nuggets faced the fifth-seeded Utah Jazz. Although the Nuggets did not win that series, they pushed the Jazz to the limit, losing four games to three in the best-of-seven series. They lost the first three games before winning

## The Name Game

The 1994 Nuggets had some interesting names on their roster. Star center Dikembe Mutombo, who was born in the Congo in central Africa, was known only by part of his name. His full name is Dikembe Mutombo Mpolondo Mukamba Jean-Jacques Wamutombo. Point guard Mahmoud Abdul-Rauf was actually born Chris Jackson, but he changed his name in 1991 when he converted to Islam. Another key player was Brian Williams, who later changed his name to Bison Dele in honor of his Native American and African roots.

three in a row to force Game 7, which host Utah took 91–81.

Denver did not win a championship that year, and it has had seasons with better regular-season records and deeper runs into the playoffs since then. But in May 1994, the Nuggets provided an exciting moment that the team's fans will not forget.

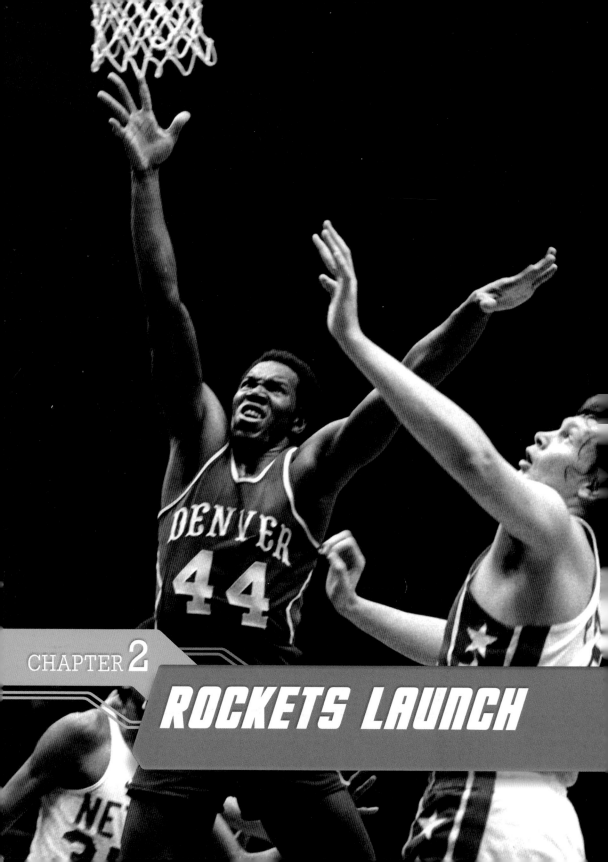

# CHAPTER 2

# ROCKETS LAUNCH

In the 1960s, the NBA was established as the major professional basketball league in the United States. Other leagues tried to compete with the NBA but failed. The NBA had all the best basketball talent.

Then, in 1967, a new league called the American Basketball Association (ABA) began play. The ABA lasted nine seasons, longer than other leagues that had attempted to compete with the NBA. The ABA survived so long because it found a way to attract talented players. The league became known for its entertaining, high-scoring games and for using a red, white, and blue ball.

## Nuggets, Part 2

The 1949–50 NBA season—the league's first season ever—featured 17 teams, including a team called the Denver Nuggets. That version of the Nuggets lasted just one season before folding, however, and it was not a very good season. The Nuggets won just 11 of their 62 games.

Ralph Simpson (44) averaged more than 20 points per game in his six seasons in Denver. He was an All-Star from 1972 to 1976.

The Rockets' Spencer Haywood drives to the basket during the American Basketball Association Western Division playoffs in May 1970.

The Denver Rockets were one of the 11 teams in the ABA's first season.

Bill Ringsby and his son Donald owned the early Rockets. The team was named after the Ringsby Rockets trucking service. The players wore orange and black uniforms.

After five years as owners, the Ringsbys sold the team. During its nine ABA seasons, the team had three ownership groups. No matter who owned the club, however, the franchise was usually one of the best in the ABA. The team made the playoffs in all nine of its ABA seasons and won the Western Division title three times.

The first true star for the Rockets was Larry Jones. The guard/forward was an ABA All-Star in each of Denver's first three seasons and led the league in scoring in 1968–69.

The Denver player who enjoyed the best season during those ABA years, however, was Spencer Haywood. Unfortunately for the Rockets, Haywood played just one season for the club. But what a season it was. Haywood was only 20 years old and had played just two seasons in college when he signed with the Rockets for the 1969–70 season. That season, he averaged 30 points and 19.5 rebounds per game. Haywood was named ABA Most Valuable Player and Rookie of the Year.

Following his remarkable season with the Rockets, Haywood signed with the NBA's Seattle SuperSonics. He continued to excel, though not quite at the same level as he had with Denver.

Denver had several other standout players in its early seasons. Ralph Simpson, a guard/forward, was a five-time All-Star. He averaged 20.4 points per game in his six seasons in Denver. Warren Jabali and Byron Beck were both two-time ABA All-Stars with Denver, and Julius Keye and Bobby Jones were two of the best defensive players in the ABA.

After the 1973–74 season, the Rockets changed their name to the Nuggets and switched

## Unsung Hero

*Denver has had several players with more star power than Byron Beck. But Beck was one of the best all-around players the franchise had in its early years. After starring at the University of Denver, he was the first player ever signed by the Rockets. The center/forward played all 10 of his professional seasons in Denver. Beck was a fan favorite. His No. 40 jersey was the first number retired by the team in 1977. Through 2010, just three other players in team history had been honored in this way.*

their team colors to blue, gold, red, and white. The team changed its name so it would not be confused with the Houston Rockets of the NBA. The nickname "Nuggets" came from the nineteenth century, when people came to Colorado to try to make a fortune by panning for gold and silver nuggets.

The Nuggets made another big change before the 1974–75 season: Larry Brown was hired as coach. He quickly helped the

## Brown's Denver History

*Larry Brown was one of the best coaches in Nuggets history, leading them to four division titles in a row from 1975 to 1978. Before becoming a coach, Brown was a top-notch point guard in the ABA. He has since become well known as a highly successful and well-traveled coach in the college and NBA ranks. Brown also played two seasons in Denver, in 1970–71 and 1971–72, and still holds team records for most assists in a game, 23, and in a half, 18.*

Nuggets become an elite team. Denver won 35 of its first 40 games with Brown as coach.

"We work hard," Simpson said. "I don't know any team that is willing to sacrifice and play together and do the things we do."

In Brown's first season as coach, the Nuggets won the five-team Western Division with a franchise-record 65 victories. The next season, the Nuggets won 60 games. They advanced to the ABA Finals but lost four games to two to Julius "Dr. J" Erving and the New York Nets. Brown was named ABA Coach of the Year in both seasons.

During the Nuggets' last season in the ABA, 1975–76, two star players joined the team. Center/forward Dan Issel, who had been a standout with the ABA's Kentucky Colonels, came to Denver. That was also the first professional

Larry Brown was named ABA Coach of the Year in his first two seasons with the Nuggets.

season for guard/forward David Thompson. One of the greatest players in team history, Thompson led Denver in scoring that season with 26 points per game. He was named ABA Rookie of the Year that season. Issel averaged 23 points a game that season.

Although the Nuggets and other ABA teams had great players, the league struggled financially. Denver's Game 6 loss to New York in the 1976 ABA Finals was the last game in league history. Most of the ABA teams went away for good. Four teams—the Nuggets, the Indiana Pacers, the New York Nets, and the San Antonio Spurs—were allowed to join the NBA.

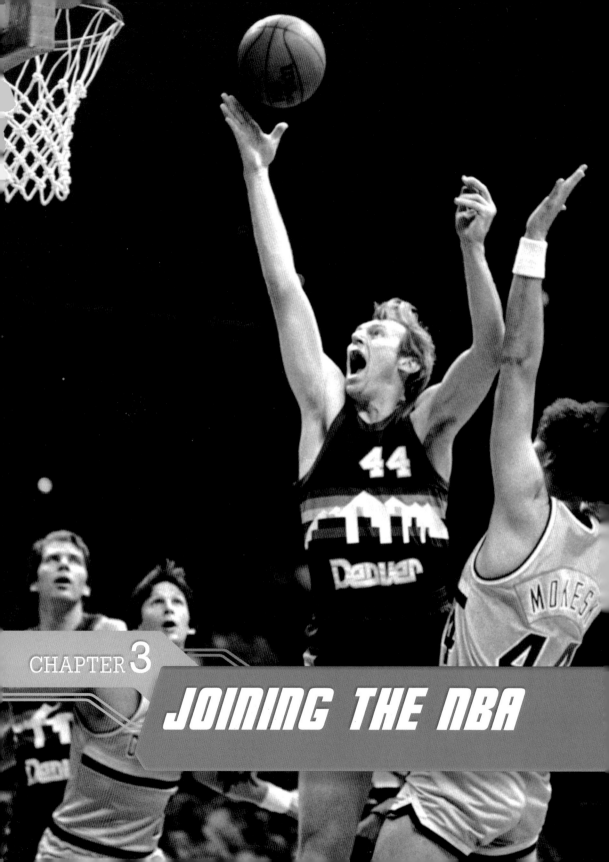

# CHAPTER 3

# JOINING THE NBA

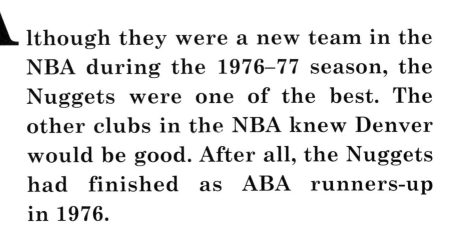

**A**lthough they were a new team in the NBA during the 1976–77 season, the Nuggets were one of the best. The other clubs in the NBA knew Denver would be good. After all, the Nuggets had finished as ABA runners-up in 1976.

"Denver has the kind of team everybody wants," Los Angeles Lakers coach Jerry West said before the 1976–77 season. "They could win it all. They're that good."

In their first season in the NBA, the Nuggets did not win the league championship. But they did have a great season,

## Popularity Rises

*When the Nuggets joined the NBA in 1976, the people of Denver got excited. The Nuggets were a great team in the ABA, but now they were joining the best basketball league in the world. Nuggets fans responded by buying 10,000 season tickets before the first season. Denver led the NBA in attendance during the team's first two seasons in the league.*

Dan Issel (44) gets into position for a rebound during a game in February 1982. Issel played 10 seasons for the Nuggets and later became their coach and general manager.

## DAN ISSEL

Before becoming a pro, Dan "The Horse" Issel, a powerfully built 6-foot-9 center/forward, starred at the University of Kentucky under legendary coach Adolph Rupp. The Detroit Pistons selected Issel in the 1970 NBA Draft, but he decided to play for the ABA's Kentucky Colonels.

Issel quickly became a star in the ABA, leading the league in scoring in his first season. Issel was named the ABA Rookie of the Year in 1971 after averaging 29.9 points and 13.2 rebounds per game. Issel helped the Colonels win the 1975 ABA title, and he was traded to the Nuggets before the next season.

Issel went on to become one of the greatest players in Nuggets history. He played 10 seasons in Denver and averaged 20.7 points and 8.3 rebounds a contest. Issel later went on to coach the Nuggets from 1992 to 1995 and then again from 1999 to 2001. He also served as general manager from 1998 to 1999.

winning their first eight games. Led by stars David Thompson, Dan Issel, and Bobby Jones, the Nuggets won the Midwest Division championship with a 50–32 record. They lost four games to two to the Portland Trail Blazers in the Western Conference playoffs. But the Nuggets proved they could play with the world's best teams.

In 1977–78, the Nuggets finished 48–34 and won a second straight Midwest Division championship. Coach Larry Brown helped them get past the Milwaukee Bucks in the first round of the playoffs. But the Nuggets lost four games to two to the Seattle SuperSonics in the conference finals.

From the start of their NBA days, the Nuggets had a reputation for being an outstanding team at home. They used Denver's high altitude

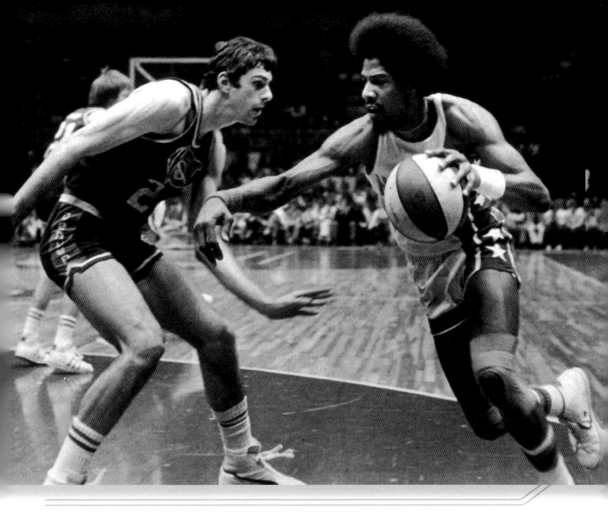

Bobby Jones defends Julius "Dr. J" Erving during the Nuggets' ABA finals game against the New Jersey Nets in May 1976.

to their advantage. Denver, known as the "Mile High City," is located 5,280 feet (1,609 m) above sea level. Breathing becomes more difficult at higher altitudes. The Nuggets were used to the environment, and they played fast-paced games at home on purpose to tire out their opponents.

In 41 regular-season home contests during their first NBA season, the Nuggets won 36. Unfortunately, the Nuggets went 14–27 away from Denver that season.

Denver had a winning home record in each of its first 14 NBA seasons. The Nuggets never could find the same results on the road, however. It was not until the 2006–07 season, their 31st in the NBA, that the Nuggets had a winning road record.

Playing in Denver was not the only advantage the Nuggets had in their first years in the NBA. They also had some marvelous players. Leading the way were Issel and Thompson, who would both be inducted into the Basketball Hall of Fame.

Even with a home-court advantage and Issel and Thompson on board, the Nuggets' run of success was about to end. Before the 1978–79 season, Denver traded Jones, who was one of the team's most popular players. Then Brown, who was the first great coach in team history, resigned on February 1, 1979, with 29 games left in the season. Donnie Walsh, who had been an assistant, took over as coach for the rest of that season.

The Nuggets made the playoffs that season but lost

## "Skywalker"

Nuggets star guard/forward David Thompson was given the nickname "Skywalker" because of his leaping ability. In college, Thompson helped lead North Carolina State to the National Collegiate Athletic Association (NCAA) title in 1974. After one more year in college, the 6-foot-4 player joined the Nuggets for their last season in the ABA and was named Rookie of the Year. Thompson also gained fame for his showdown with Julius "Dr. J" Erving in the Slam Dunk Contest at the 1976 ABA All-Star Game in Denver. Erving won the contest, the first of its kind in pro basketball. But both players amazed the fans. Thompson averaged 24.1 points per game in his seven seasons with Denver. He finished his career, which was cut short by off-the-court troubles, by playing two seasons with the Seattle SuperSonics.

The Nuggets' David Thompson, *left*, eyes his target against the New York Nets in January 1976. Thompson averaged more than 24 points per game in seven seasons with the Nuggets.

in the first round. The next season, with Walsh as coach, the Nuggets won just 30 of 82 games. They did not make the postseason for the first time in their history. The Nuggets also got off to a bad start in the 1980–81 season and missed the playoffs again.

The 1980–81 campaign, however, was a turning point. Walsh coached just 31 games that season before Doug Moe replaced him. During the next decade with Moe as coach, the Nuggets were one of the most consistently strong teams in the NBA.

# CHAPTER 4

# MOE'S TEAM

At the Pepsi Center, where the Nuggets have played since 1999, banners hang from the rafters to honor four great players from the team's history—Alex English (No. 2), David Thompson (No. 33), Byron Beck (No. 40), and Dan Issel (No. 44).

Another banner, with the number 432, hangs high above the court. That banner honors the winningest coach in Nuggets history—Doug Moe. From 1980 to 1990, Moe was the Nuggets' coach. He won 432 games and lost 357.

"He has meant so much to the Denver community," Kiki Vandeweghe said on the night Moe was honored in 2002. Vandeweghe played for Moe and was the Nuggets' general manager in 2002.

Moe was one of the most colorful characters in team history. He was known as a bad dresser, but he joked about it. "My only rule is that you have

Alex English is the Nuggets' all-time leading scorer with 21,645 points. His jersey number, 2, has been retired by the team.

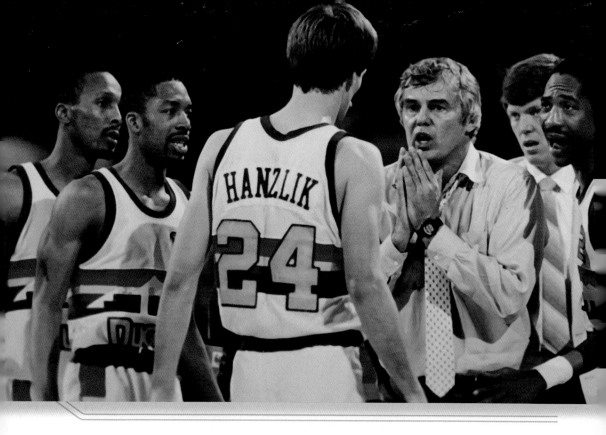

Spirited coach Doug Moe turned the Nuggets into an offensive power in the 1980s. The Nuggets led the NBA in scoring during six of his 10 seasons with the team.

## What a Stiff

*Nuggets coach Doug Moe, known as the "Big Stiff," was famous for referring to most players as a "stiff," meaning that the player was not anybody special. "He called everybody a stiff," said T. R. Dunn, a guard/forward who played parts of 10 seasons with the Nuggets from 1980 to 1990. "He'd call star players on other teams stiffs to try to help motivate you to play them tougher."*

to dress better than me to be acceptable," he once said. Moe was loved by fans and players. But most of Moe's former players also remember his temper, which during games was nearly unmatched.

An interesting personality was not what defined Moe, however. Rather, it was the

Nuggets' run of success under his guidance. When Moe, who had been an assistant coach with the team, took over as head coach 31 games into the 1980–81 season, the Nuggets were 11–20. They went 26–25 the rest of the way with him in charge. The Nuggets did not reach the playoffs that season. But that was only time they missed the postseason with Moe as coach.

In nine full seasons as coach from 1981 to 1990, Moe led the Nuggets to nine play-off appearances. They won the Midwest Division title in 1985 and 1988. Moe was named NBA Coach of the Year for the 1987–88 season.

Those Nuggets teams were known for their exciting offenses. Leading the way was English, who throughout Moe's decade as coach was one of the NBA's greatest scorers.

But English was not Denver's only productive offensive player. Issel, Thompson, and Vandeweghe could also score. Michael Adams, Walter Davis, Lafayette "Fat" Lever, and Calvin Natt had big statistical seasons under Moe, too.

It is fitting that Moe's Nuggets are a part of NBA history. The Nuggets and the Detroit Pistons played the highest-scoring game in league history on December 13, 1983, at McNichols Arena in Denver. Detroit prevailed 186–184 in triple overtime. Five players

# A QUIET STAR

No conversation about the greatest players in Nuggets history could be complete without Alex English.

English was a standout at the University of South Carolina before the Milwaukee Bucks drafted him in 1976. The lanky 6-foot-7 forward played two unremarkable seasons in Milwaukee before he signed with the Indiana Pacers. English began to score more points, but it was not until he was traded to Denver during the 1979–80 season that he developed into a star.

While with the Nuggets, English became known for his elegant style of play, his midrange shooting ability, and his unassuming way of doing his job. He led the NBA in scoring during the 1982–83 season at 28.4 points per game. English averaged at least 25 points in eight straight seasons, from 1981–82 to 1988–89. Through the 2010–11 season, his 21,645 points ranked first in club history.

scored at least 35 points, led by Vandeweghe's 51.

English, who had 47 points in that contest against Detroit, said he loved the Nuggets' style of play when Moe was their coach. "Oh, it was great. That was basketball at its finest," English said.

Denver led the NBA in scoring five straight seasons, from 1980–81 through 1984–85, and then again in 1987–88. Through the 2010–11 season, the 1981–82 Nuggets' average of 126.5 points per game was still the NBA record.

During Moe's decade, the Nuggets reached their peak in 1984–85. That season, they went 52–30 and won the Midwest Division title. In the playoffs, they beat the San Antonio Spurs and the Utah Jazz to get to the Western Conference finals. The

Kiki Vandeweghe (55) drives to the basket past the Kansas City Kings' Larry Drew (22) in January 1984.

Nuggets lost four games to one to the Los Angeles Lakers in the conference finals.

The Nuggets advanced to the second round of the postseason three other times in the 1980s—in 1983, 1986, and 1988—but lost each time. After the 1990 season, the Nuggets went through several changes. The team had new owners, and they hired Bernie Bickerstaff as general manager. Bickerstaff, the owners, and Moe all agreed at that point that it was time for Moe to leave.

"After 10 years, it's tough to leave the people you're close to," Moe said. "I'll be able to be a fan for a while. I don't know if I'll ever get back into coaching."

Moe never again became a head coach.

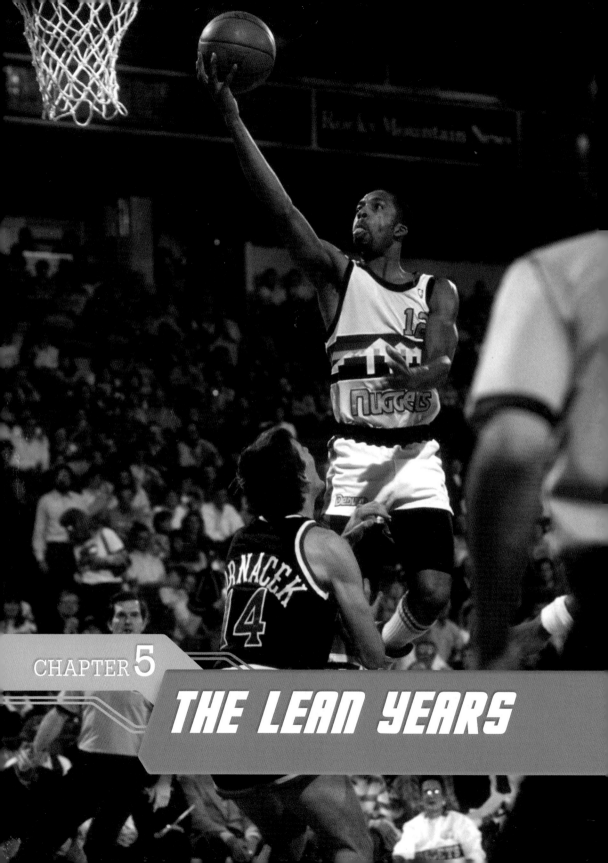

# CHAPTER 5

# THE LEAN YEARS

**T**he summer of 1990 marked the beginning of a new, downward direction for the Nuggets. For years, Denver had been a team that made the playoffs nearly every season. In fact, the Nuggets had made the postseason nine straight years with Doug Moe as coach.

Forward Alex English, guard/forward Bill Hanzlik, guard Lafayette "Fat" Lever, and center/forward Danny Schayes were key Nuggets for most of those nine seasons.

That summer, Moe left the Nuggets and so did those four key players. Schayes was traded to the Milwaukee Bucks. Lever was dealt to the Dallas Mavericks. Hanzlik retired. Even English was gone that summer. He signed with Dallas and played one more NBA season before retiring.

For Nuggets fans, it was the hardest to see English go.

Guard Lafayette "Fat" Lever was part of the Nuggets' playoff success, but he was traded to the Dallas Mavericks prior to the 1990-91 season.

He appeared in more games than any other player in team history. He also scored more points than any player in team history.

But 1990 was the start of something new for Denver. Paul Westhead, who had been coaching in the college ranks at Loyola Marymount in California, replaced Moe as coach. He brought a high-scoring offense with him. This made Nuggets games exciting, but the team did not win very often.

Led by standouts Michael Adams, Orlando Woolridge, Walter Davis, Reggie Williams, and Chris Jackson (who later changed his name to Mahmoud Abdul-Rauf), the Nuggets were the NBA's highest-scoring team in the 1990–91 season. They averaged 119.9 points per game. They were also the league's poorest defensive team, however, giving up an average of 130.8 points. This set an NBA defensive record. As a result, they finished 20–62.

From 1990 to 2003, the Nuggets were one of the worst teams in the NBA. Denver made the playoffs just two times during that span—in 1994 and 1995.

The 1993–94 season provided the Nuggets with some

## Mighty Mite

Michael Adams was just 5 feet 10 inches tall, but he had a big shot. Adams, who played for the Nuggets from 1987 to 1991, was one of the most successful three-point shooters in team history. He made a three-pointer in 79 consecutive games from January 1988 to January 1989. This set an NBA record that was later broken. Adams attempted the second-most three-pointers (1,841) of any player in team history and led Denver in scoring, with 26.5 points per game, in 1990–91. Adams was also a skilled passer. Through the 2010–11 season, Alex English and Fat Lever were the only players in team history with more assists.

The Nuggets' Michael Adams scoots past New York Knicks guard Mark Jackson in January 1991.

hope. It was during that season's playoffs that they became the first number eight seed to win a postseason series in defeating the top-seeded Seattle SuperSonics. Denver then nearly upset Utah in the second round, taking the Jazz to seven games before falling. Leading that team was a group of young players, including Abdul-Rauf, Reggie Williams, Brian Williams, Dikembe Mutombo, LaPhonso Ellis, Robert Pack, and Bryant Stith.

Unfortunately for Nuggets fans, those young stars did not last long in Denver. By the summer of 1996, Mutombo, Abdul-Rauf, Brian Williams,

Reggie Williams, and Pack were gone. Ellis left two years later, and Stith left in 2000.

Another glimmer of hope appeared before the 1998–99 season as power forward Antonio McDyess signed with Denver. He had played for the Nuggets from 1995 to 1997 but was traded to the Phoenix Suns. After one season in Phoenix, he returned to Denver.

"As we get better as a team, more people will recognize Antonio," said Dan Issel, who was the Nuggets' general manager at the time. "Talentwise and as a physical specimen, he's up there with anyone."

The Nuggets did not get much better as a team, however. They never made the playoffs with McDyess, and changes around the team kept happening. From 1989 to 2000, the Nuggets had five different ownership groups. From 1990

## The Lowest Point

*The worst season in Nuggets history was the 1997–98 campaign, in which Denver went 11–71. That season, former Nuggets player Bill Hanzlik coached the team. Many of the best players of previous years had been traded or let go by management, so Hanzlik did not have much to work with. Among the five longest losing streaks in team history through 2009–10, three came during the 1997–98 season—including a team-record 23 consecutive losses. The Nuggets also lost the first 12 games of the season.*

to 2003, the Nuggets had 10 coaching changes. The team went through a lot of different players, too.

Going into the 2002–03 season, the Nuggets were facing the prospect of yet another bad season. They had won just 27 games the season before and did not appear to be any better now. New coach Jeff Bzdelik knew it would take a while for Denver to become good again.

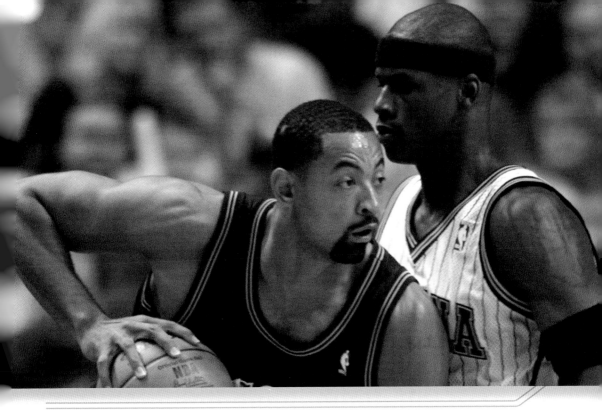

Nuggets forward Juwan Howard, *left*, was one of the few bright spots for the team during the 2002–03 season. He averaged more than 18 points per game that season.

"I know that what we're doing here is going to work someday," Bzdelik said before that season, "and hopefully I'll be here to see it when it does."

It did not work in 2002–03. The Nuggets went 17–65, the second-worst season in team history. It was a low point for Denver. But a high point was just around the corner.

## A New Owner

*After going through several owners in a short period of time throughout the 1990s, the Nuggets gained some stability in 2000. That year, E. Stanley Kroenke purchased not only the Nuggets but the Colorado Avalanche hockey team as well. As of 2011, Kroenke still owned both teams and the Pepsi Center, the arena in which both teams play.*

# CHAPTER 6

# "MELO" ARRIVES

# The Denver Nuggets had a poor season in 2002–03. The good news was that their record helped them land the third pick in the 2003 NBA Draft.

On the night of June 26, 2003, the Nuggets used that pick to take Carmelo Anthony from Syracuse University. Anthony led Syracuse to college basketball's national championship just two months earlier. The Nuggets believed the 6-foot-8 forward, nicknamed "Melo," could lead them to great things, too.

About a month later, the Nuggets signed free-agent point guard Andre Miller. Then they signed guards Earl Boykins, Jon Barry, and Voshon Lenard. That group was added to big men Marcus Camby and Nene

Carmelo Anthony made an immediate impact in Denver. He played in the NBA Rookie Challenge in February 2004 and gave fans a treat with his acrobatic dunks.

Hilario, who became Nuggets a year earlier. Suddenly, Denver had a good basketball team.

"I look forward to playing with guys who want to get better and want to win," Miller said.

The addition of Miller, who had played for the Cleveland Cavaliers and the Los Angeles Clippers, was a boost for the Nuggets. But Anthony made the biggest splash. He was Denver's newest star. That was clear from the start.

Although just 19 years old, Anthony averaged 21 points and 6.1 rebounds per game as a rookie. Most importantly, he turned Denver around. After winning 17 games the season before, the Nuggets went 43–39 in Anthony's rookie campaign. That was good enough to get Denver to the playoffs for the first time in nine years.

"I did what I had to do on the court," Anthony said. "We're in the playoffs. I think anybody who is home would rather be in the situation I am right now."

Denver was the number eight seed and lost four games to one to the top-seeded Minnesota Timberwolves in the first round. But things were looking up for the Nuggets. Before the next season, they added another key piece to the puzzle. They acquired power forward Kenyon

## "Melo" Gives Back

Carmelo Anthony quickly emerged as one of the NBA's top scorers. Through the 2009–10 campaign, he had averaged more than 25 points per game in four different seasons with the Nuggets, including a career-high 28.9 in 2006–07. Fans in Denver also loved him because of his charity work. He hosted an annual holiday party for kids called "A Very Melo Christmas." He also donated millions of dollars during his career and purchased countless tickets to Nuggets games for less fortunate families.

Andre Miller maintains control of the ball against the Sacramento Kings' Mike Bibby in November 2004.

Martin, who had starred for the New Jersey Nets, in a trade for two first-round draft choices.

Still, the Nuggets felt they needed something else to take another step forward. They got that something else on January 27, 2005, when they named George Karl as coach. Karl was a longtime NBA coach who had enjoyed his greatest success when he was in charge

## The Iverson Experiment

In 2006, the Nuggets were looking for a spark. They got one when they traded Andre Miller to the Philadelphia 76ers in a multiplayer deal and got Allen Iverson in return. At the time, Iverson was one of the NBA's biggest stars. Iverson, who was an explosive scorer despite being just 6 feet tall, averaged more than 25 points per game with Denver and made the All-Star team twice. But the Nuggets were only 1–8 in playoff games with Iverson.

Coach George Karl brought a needed turnaround to the Nuggets' 2004–05 season. The Nuggets won 32 of their last 40 games to make the playoffs.

of the Seattle SuperSonics. He replaced Jeff Bzdelik, who had been fired a month earlier.

Before Karl was named coach, the Nuggets were struggling. Despite having Anthony, Miller, Martin, and other talented players, they started the 2004–05 season with a 17–25 record. After Karl took over as coach, the Nuggets won 32 of their last 40 games to reach the playoffs again.

"[Karl] put the fun back in the game for me," Anthony said. "He motivated me to go out there and have fun."

Karl sent a surge of energy into the Nuggets, but it still took a while to get them to that next level. Denver lost in the first round of the 2005 playoffs and for the next three years as well. This gave the Nuggets a five-season streak (2004 to 2008) of exiting in the postseason's opening round.

In the 2005–06 season, the Nuggets won the Northwest Division with a 44–38 record but fell to the Clippers in five games in the first round of the playoffs. During the next season, the Nuggets acquired 76ers star guard Allen Iverson in a multiplayer deal in which Denver sent Miller to the 76ers. Even with Iverson, though, the Nuggets continued to fall in the opening round of the playoffs.

The 2008–09 season was another turning point for Denver. Three games into that season, the Nuggets made a big change. They traded Iverson to the Detroit Pistons and got Chauncey Billups in return.

Billups, a point guard, grew up in Denver and was a star at the University of Colorado before entering the NBA. Billups was in his 12th NBA season and had helped Detroit win the NBA title in 2004. Denver fans loved having Billups come home. Billups loved it, too.

"Being here, it's priceless," he said. "It really is a dream come true."

The Nuggets believed Billups provided the leadership and winning attitude the team needed. "What I've felt from

## Hometown Hero

Chauncey Billups was already well known in Denver before the Nuggets acquired him in 2008 from the Detroit Pistons. He won two state championships with Denver's George Washington High School. After high school, he went to the University of Colorado and led the Buffaloes to the NCAA tournament. He was with the Nuggets early in his NBA career, from 1998 to 2000, before he played for the Minnesota Timberwolves and Detroit.

him as much as any player I've coached in Denver is winning," Karl said. "It's winning and nothing else."

Winning is exactly what the Nuggets did. With Anthony and Billups leading the way, the Nuggets finished 54–28 and won the Northwest Division. Denver then cruised past the New Orleans Hornets in five games in the first round of the playoffs. It was the first time the Nuggets had won a postseason series in 15 years—since the win over the Sonics in 1994.

Then the Nuggets beat the Dallas Mavericks four games to one to get to the Western Conference finals. They had not been in that round since 1985. Awaiting Denver in the conference finals were the mighty Los Angeles Lakers. The Nuggets gave the Lakers a battle, but Kobe Bryant led the Lakers to a four-games-to-two series victory. "I'll never forget this year," Billups said. "But this is not as far as I want to go."

After the memorable 2008–09 season, the Nuggets had high hopes going into 2009–10. They finished 53–29, won a second consecutive Northwest Division crown, and made a seventh straight trip to the playoffs. However, Denver fell four games to two to the Utah Jazz in the first round.

"It got a little frustrating at times," Anthony said. "I'm proud of my guys for fighting out there. The energy, the effort—it was out there. Everything we asked for was given on the court."

Since Anthony arrived in the summer of 2003, the Nuggets had been among the NBA's top teams. But Anthony was to be a free agent in the summer of 2011. Rather than lose him in free agency, the

The Nuggets' Chauncey Billups, *right*, fends off Dallas Mavericks guard Jerry Stackhouse in a November 2008 game.

Nuggets traded Anthony, Billups, and three other players to the New York Knicks on February 22, 2011. Wilson Chandler, Raymond Felton, and Danilo Gallinari all arrived in Denver as part of the three-team trade. All are former first-round NBA Draft picks.

After the trade, the Nuggets came together and continued to win with an amped up defense. The team finished the regular season with a strong 50–32 record and moved on to face the Oklahoma City Thunder in the first round of the playoffs. However, Denver lost the series four games to one.

Although their exciting second-half run ended in the playoffs, Denver was optimistic that its new cast of players could someday bring the city a championship.

# TIMELINE

| | |
|---|---|
| **1967** | The Denver Rockets debut in the ABA. |
| **1970** | The Rockets win the ABA's Western Division. It was the first of 10 division championships, through 2009–10, for the franchise. The team was led by rookie forward/center Spencer Haywood, who was selected ABA MVP. |
| **1974** | After seven seasons as the Rockets, the team changes its name and colors. In honor of the Colorado gold rush in the 1800s, the franchise becomes the Nuggets. |
| **1976** | Shortly after losing to the Nets, the Nuggets become one of four ABA teams to join the NBA. The others are the Nets, the Indiana Pacers, and the San Antonio Spurs. |
| **1977** | The Nuggets finish their first NBA season 50–32 and win the Midwest Division championship. |
| **1980** | Assistant Doug Moe takes over as head coach of the Nuggets in December, replacing the fired Donnie Walsh. Moe would become the winningest coach in team history with a 432–357 record and lead the team to nine straight playoff appearances from 1982–90. |
| **1983** | In the highest-scoring game in NBA history, the Nuggets fall 186–184 to the visiting Detroit Pistons in three overtimes on December 13. Denver's Kiki Vandeweghe scores a game-high 51 points, and teammate Alex English adds 47. |
| **1985** | The Nuggets average 120 points per game in the 1984–85 campaign, leading the NBA in scoring for a fifth straight season. |

**1990**

English plays his last game in a Nuggets uniform, scoring 23 points in Denver's 115–108 home win over the Minnesota Timberwolves on April 22. English ends his Nuggets career as the team's all-time leading scorer with 21,645 points.

**1994**

The Nuggets make NBA history. After finishing the regular season 42–40 to qualify for the playoffs, they become the first number eight seed to beat a top seed, upsetting the Seattle SuperSonics three games to two.

**2003**

Following a season in which the Nuggets finish 17–65, the team drafts Syracuse University star forward Carmelo Anthony with the third pick in the NBA Draft on June 26.

**2004**

In his first season, Anthony averages 21 points and 6.1 rebounds per game and leads the Nuggets to a 43–39 record and their first playoff appearance in nine years. Denver, the number eight seed, falls in five games to the Timberwolves in the first round.

**2005**

George Karl, a longtime NBA coach for several teams, is named coach of the Nuggets in late January. Under his direction, the team wins 32 of its final 40 regular-season games to finish 49–33. Denver loses four games to one to the Spurs in the first round of the playoffs.

**2009**

Led by Karl, Anthony, and Chauncey Billups, the Nuggets win the Northwest Division title and advance to the NBA's Western Conference finals for the third time. Denver loses to the Los Angeles Lakers in six games.

**2011**

The Nuggets trade Anthony, Billups, and three other players to the New York Knicks in a three-team deal on February 22.

# QUICK STATS

## FRANCHISE HISTORY

Denver Rockets (1967–74)
Denver Nuggets (1974– )

## NBA FINALS
*(1977– )*

None

## ABA FINALS
*(1967–76)*

1976

## CONFERENCE FINALS

1978, 1985, 2009

## DIVISION CHAMPIONSHIPS

1977, 1978, 1985, 1988, 2006, 2009, 2010

## KEY PLAYERS
*(position[s]; seasons with team)*

Carmelo Anthony (F; 2003–11)
Byron Beck (C/F; 1967–77)
Chauncey Billups (G; 1999–2000, 2008–11)
T. R. Dunn (G/F; 1980–90)
Alex English (F; 1980–90)
Bill Hanzlik (G/F; 1982–90)
Dan Issel (C/F; 1975–85)
Bobby Jones (F; 1974–78)
Fat Lever (G; 1984–90)
Dikembe Mutombo (C; 1991–96)
Ralph Simpson (G/F; 1970–76, 1978)
David Thompson (G/F; 1975–82)
Kiki Vandeweghe (F; 1980–84)

## KEY COACHES

Larry Brown (1974–79):
    251–134; 21–24 (postseason)
George Karl (2005– ):
    278–172; 15–26 (postseason)
Doug Moe (1980–90):
    432–357; 24–37 (postseason)

## HOME ARENAS

Denver Auditorium Arena (1967–75)
McNichols Sports Arena (1975–99)
Pepsi Center (1999– )

* All statistics through 2010–11 season

# QUOTES AND ANECDOTES

The three most successful coaches in Nuggets history are Larry Brown, George Karl, and Doug Moe. Their success in Denver is not the only thing that connects them, however. All three of them played their college basketball at the University of North Carolina. Brown and Moe were college teammates.

"He tried to get the most out of everybody. But after the game, it was like a total transformation. He was this happy-go-lucky guy after the game. You would be wondering if this is the same person that one or two minutes ago was screaming at you the whole game." —Former Nuggets guard/forward T. R. Dunn, on coach Doug Moe

Guard Lafayette "Fat" Lever, who played for the Nuggets from 1984 to 1990, had 43 career triple-doubles. A triple-double is a game in which a player reaches double digits in three different statistical categories (points, rebounds, assists, steals, or blocked shots). Through the 2010–11 season, Lever's total ranked sixth in NBA history. Oscar Robertson had the most triple-doubles with 181, followed by Magic Johnson with 138.

David Thompson was a great player, and he was never better than on April 9, 1978. That night in Detroit, he scored 73 points in the Nuggets' 139–137 loss to the Pistons in both teams' regular-season finale. Thompson had 32 points in the first quarter alone. Through 2010, only two players in NBA history had scored more points in a game that did not go into overtime. The Philadelphia Warriors' Wilt Chamberlain scored 100 in a game in March 1962, and the Los Angeles Lakers' Kobe Bryant had 81 in a game in January 2006.

# GLOSSARY

**assist**

A pass that leads directly to a made basket.

**decade**

A period of 10 years.

**draft**

A system used by professional sports leagues to select new players in order to spread incoming talent among all teams. The NBA Draft is held each June.

**emerge**

To become noticed.

**franchise**

An entire sports organization, including the players, coaches, and staff.

**free agent**

A player whose contract has expired and who is able to sign with a team of his choice.

**general manager**

The executive who is in charge of the team's overall operation. He or she hires and fires managers and coaches, drafts players, and signs free agents.

**hoist**

To raise or lift something.

**motivate**

To cause someone to do well.

**resign**

To give up a job or position.

**retire**

To officially end one's career.

**roster**

The players as a whole on a team.

**trade**

A move in which a player or players are sent from one team to another.

**veteran**

An individual with great experience in a particular endeavor.

# FOR MORE INFORMATION

## Further Reading

Anthony, Carmelo, and Greg Brown. *Carmelo Anthony: It's Just the Beginning.* Kirkland, WA: Positively for Kids, 2004.

Ballard, Chris. *The Art of a Beautiful Game: The Thinking Fan's Tour of the NBA.* New York: Simon & Schuster, 2009.

Simmons, Bill. *The Book of Basketball: The NBA According to the Sports Guy.* New York: Random House, 2009.

## Web Links

To learn more about the Denver Nuggets, visit ABDO Publishing Company online at **www.abdopublishing.com**. Web sites about the Nuggets are featured on our Book Links page. These links are routinely monitored and updated to provide the most current information available.

## Places to Visit

**Colorado Sports Hall of Fame**
INVESCO Field at Mile High
1701 Bryant Street, Suite 500
Denver, CO 80204
720-258-3888
www.coloradosports.org
This hall of fame honors individuals for their athletic accomplishments in Colorado. Former Nuggets players Alex English, Bill Hanzlik, and Dan Issel are among those enshrined here.

**Naismith Memorial Basketball Hall of Fame**
1000 West Columbus Avenue
Springfield, MA 01105
413-781-6500
www.hoophall.com
This hall of fame highlights the greatest players in the history of basketball. Alex English, Dan Issel, and David Thompson and coach Larry Brown are among the inductees.

**Pepsi Center**
1000 Chopper Circle
Denver, CO 80204
303-405-1100
www.pepsicenter.com
This has been the Nuggets' home arena since 1999. The team plays 41 regular-season games here each season.

# INDEX

Abdul-Rauf, Mahmoud, 6, 8–9, 30, 31
Adams, Michael, 25, 30
Anthony, Carmelo, 35, 36, 38, 40–41

Barry, Jon, 35
Beck, Byron, 13, 23
Bickerstaff, Bernie (general manager), 27
Billups, Chauncey, 39–40, 41
Boykins, Earl, 35
Brown, Larry (coach), 14, 18, 20, 25
Bzdelik, Jeff (coach), 32–33, 38

Camby, Marcus, 35
Chandler, Wilson, 41

Dallas Mavericks, 29, 40
Davis, Walter, 25, 30
Denver Rockets, 12–13
Detroit Pistons, 18, 25, 26, 39
Dunn, T. R., 24

Ellis, LaPhonso, 6, 7, 8, 31, 32
English, Alex, 23, 25, 26, 29, 30

Felton, Raymond, 41

Gallinari, Danilo, 41

Hanzlik, Bill, 29, 32
Haywood, Spencer, 13
Hilario, Nene, 35–36

Issel, Dan (player and coach), 6, 8, 9, 14–15, 18, 20, 23, 25, 32
Iverson, Allen, 37, 39

Jabali, Warren, 13
Jones, Bobby, 13, 18, 20
Jones, Larry, 12–13

Karl, George (coach), 8, 37–38, 39–40
Keye, Julius, 13
Kroenke, E. Stanley (owner), 33

Lenard, Voshon, 35
Lever, Lafayette "Fat," 25, 29, 30
Los Angeles Lakers, 17, 27, 40

Martin, Kenyon, 36–37, 38
McDyess, Antonio, 32
McNichols Arena, 25
Miller, Andre, 35, 36, 37, 38, 39
Milwaukee Bucks, 18, 26, 29
Moe, Doug (coach), 21, 23–27, 29, 30
Mutombo, Dikembe, 5, 6, 7, 8–9, 31

Natt, Calvin, 25

Pack, Robert, 8, 31, 32
Pepsi Center, 23, 33

Ringsby, Bill (owner), 12
Ringsby, Donald (owner), 12
Rogers, Rodney, 6

San Antonio Spurs, 15, 26
Schayes, Danny, 29
Seattle SuperSonics, 5–8, 13, 18, 20, 31, 38, 40
Simpson, Ralph, 13, 14
Stith, Bryant, 6, 8, 31, 32

Thompson, David "Skywalker," 15, 18, 20, 23, 25

Utah Jazz, 9, 26, 31, 40

Vandeweghe, Kiki, 23, 25, 26

Walsh, Donnie (coach), 20–21
Westhead, Paul, 30
Williams, Brian, 6, 8, 9, 31
Williams, Reggie, 6–7, 8, 30, 31, 32
Woolridge, Orlando, 30

## About the Author

Brian Howell, a freelance writer based in Denver, Colorado, has written several books about sports. He has been a sports journalist for more than 17 years, writing about high school, college, and professional athletics. He has covered major sporting events such as the U.S. Open golf tournament, the World Series, the Stanley Cup playoffs, and the NBA All-Star Game. He has earned several writing awards during his career. The Colorado native lives with his wife and four children.